SPECIAL EDITION
HAPPY BIRTHDAY, ANGLO-SAXON TIMES
650 YEARS OLD TODAY

Anglo-Saxon Times

3rd January, AD 1060

Andrew Langley

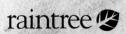
raintree

a Capstone company — publishers for children

Raintree is an imprint of Capstone Global Library Limited, a company incorporated in England and Wales having its registered office at 264 Banbury Road, Oxford, OX2 7DY – Registered company number: 6695582

www.raintree.co.uk
myorders@raintree.co.uk

Edited by Helen Cox Cannons
Designed by Philippa Jenkins
Illustrated by Philippa Jenkins
Picture research by Tracy Cummins and Ruth Smith
Originated by Capstone Global Library Ltd
Produced by Victoria Fitzgerald
Printed and bound in China

ISBN 978 1 4747 3254 3
21 20 19 18 17
10 9 8 7 6 5 4 3 2 1

British Library Cataloguing in Publication Data
A full catalogue record for this book is available from the British Library.

Acknowledgements
We would like to thank the following for permission to reproduce photographs: Alamy: Archimage, 22 Top, epa european pressphoto agency b.v., 20, History Pictures, 5 Top, Holmes Garden Photos, 14, 16, INTERFOTO, 26, 28 Middle Left, Jeff Morgan 05, 10, Les Gibbon, 12, Timewatch Images, 28 Top Left, World History Archive, 18 Left, 27; Capstone Press: Cover Middle, 4 Bottom, 5 Bottom, 6, 7, 9 Bottom, Philippa Jenkins, Design elements, 1, 15, 29, Steve Mead, Cover Top Left, 4 Top; Dreamstime: Michael Foley, 8; Getty Images: Culture Club, 13, Museum of London/Heritage Images, 28 Right; iStockphoto: dan_wrench, Cover Bottom Left, 21; ©Marco Simola: photographersdirect.com, 11; Shutterstock: 1000 Words, 22 Bottom, Anna Hoychuk, 28 Middle, Baimieng, 25 Left, BERNATSKAYA OXANA, 28 Bottom, Carolyn Franks, 19 Bottom Left, Eugene Sergeev, 18 Right, Ivaschenko Roman, 19 Bottom Right, Kachalkina Veronika, Cover Bottom Right, 24 Bottom Right, 24 Top, Khosro, Cover Top Right, 17, Lokuttara, Cover Bottom Middle, Nejron Photo, Cover Middle Right, 24 Bottom Left, Nicram Sabod, Cover Middle Background, 9 Top, Peter Lorimer, 25, Picsfive, Cover Bottom Middle Background, PlusONE, 25 Right, Ron Zmiri, 4 Bottom, Sinelev, 19 Top Left, SueC, Cover Middle Right Background, TTphoto, 23 Right, Valentin Agapov, Design elements, Veronika Synenko, Cover Bottom Middle, Victor Maschek, 23 Left.

We would like to thank Dr Linsey Hunter at the University of the Highlands and Islands for her invaluable help in the preparation of this book.

Inside...

Some words are shown in bold, **like this**. You can find out what they mean by looking in the glossary.

read on...

Happy Birthday to us!

Editor Hilda Hardnose writes:

Wilcuma! (If you don't speak Old English, that means "Welcome!"). Here is a special birthday edition of the *Anglo-Saxon Times*. It's 650 years old this year!

A lot has happened during that time. To start with, in AD 410, the Romans packed up and left Britain. But soon other people landed on our shores – Angles and Saxons, speaking a strange language. After them came the terrifying Vikings, who conquered large parts of Britain. But even the Vikings settled down in the end. Who knows what will happen next?

To celebrate our 650th anniversary, we've put together a selection of our all-time favourite news stories. They are organized by subject, and you can find the dates beside each article. We hope you enjoy this look back at the past – and the present!

WE'RE ON OUR OWN!

Romans scarper

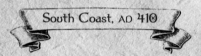
South Coast, AD 410

Britain is in big trouble. Law and order is breaking down. Bands of Picts are sweeping down from the north. Germanic tribes are invading from the east. Who is going to protect us?

Well, not the Roman army for a start. They've all gone. Today the last of the legions sailed away across the Channel. For the first time in nearly 370 years, there are no Roman soldiers in Britain.

The Roman commander, Constantine, told the *Times*:

"We're needed in Gaul. Things are even worse over there. So you'll have to look after yourselves."

GAELIC PALS

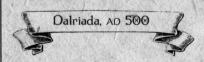
Dalriada, AD 500

Say hello to a grand new kingdom. Dalriada stretches across the few kilometres of sea between north-east Ireland and western Scotland. The Irish and Scots peoples on both sides have united under a single leader, King Fergus. They also speak the same language: **Gaelic**.

Dalriada
Irish/Scots

Scotland

Ireland

WHO ARE ALL THESE PEOPLE?

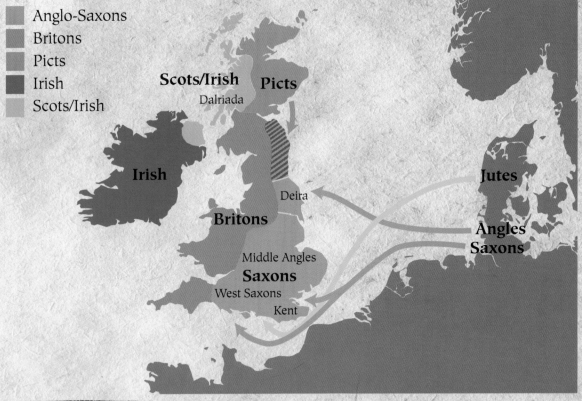

- Anglo-Saxons
- Britons
- Picts
- Irish
- Scots/Irish

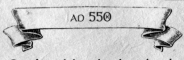
AD 550

Confused by the boatloads of settlers who have arrived on our shores? They speak weird languages and wear strange clothes. And they're changing our islands forever.

Here's your cut-out-and-keep guide to the Angles, Saxons and all the other folk in the great British mixing pot.

From Germany
Angles, who live mainly on the east coast of England, from Northumbria down to Essex

Saxons have moved in to Sussex (named after the "South Saxons") and Wessex ("West Saxons")

From Denmark
Jutes, who live in Kent and southern England

From Scotland
Picts, who ruled most of Scotland, but also attacked Northumbria

From Ireland
Scots or Gaels, who have settled on the west coast of – guess where – Scotland

From England
Britons, who have migrated to Wales (including Cornwall)

DANE AND OUT!
Alfred's amazing triumph

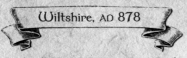
Wiltshire, AD 878

At last! The Great Army of the **Danes**, led by Guthrum, has been beaten at the Battle of Edington. King Alfred and his soldiers have driven them out of Wessex after a stunning victory.

The Great Army landed in Britain 13 years ago. It rampaged up and down the east coast, then made a surprise attack in the south. And now Alfred has gathered a large force and defeated the invaders at Edington. The Danes still rule much of east and north-east England – but Wessex belongs to King Alfred.

Why did Alfred win?
General Basham-Uppe, our defence correspondent, writes:

"That Alfred's a cunning chap. While his army was small and weak he hid in the wild marshes of Somerset. This spring he rode out and called together men from all over Wessex. Then his army was much bigger and stronger than the Danes."

RELIGIOUS NEWS

BURYING A SHIP

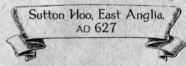

Sutton Hoo, East Anglia, AD 627

Ships on the sea? OK. But a ship under the ground?

No wonder huge crowds gathered at Sutton Hoo, East Anglia, this week. They had come to see the funeral of their old ruler, King Raedwald. Long ago, his **ancestors** had sailed to Britain in a **longship**. Now he was being buried in one – on land.

It was an amazing sight. The king's body lay in the middle of the ship. Packed around the body were glittering treasures, including gold jewellery, silver ornaments, **bronze** dishes and beautiful armour. Then the whole thing was covered with a huge mound of earth.

One mourner said:

"Nobody will ever see these wonderful objects again. Sad, innit?"

RELIGIOUS NEWS

HOLY HOME ON LINDISFARNE

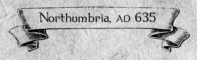
Northumbria, AD 635

A new island monastery

It's tiny. It's deserted. It's peaceful. And it's cut off by the tide twice a day. This makes it just the place for monks to live!

Irish holy man Aidan is heading for Lindisfarne, off England's north-east coast. Aidan was invited by King Oswald of Northumbria. Aidan's mission is to build a **monastery** on this lovely island. He hopes it will become a major centre of Christian prayer and learning.

MONKS FLEE HOLY ISLAND

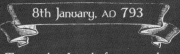
8th January, AD 793

Terror hit Lindisfarne today. Viking raiders attacked the island, destroying the church, stealing treasure and killing the inhabitants. But it wasn't a complete surprise:

"The warning signs were all there," said one monk. *"Lately we've seen whirlwinds, lightning and fiery dragons in the sky."*

BUSINESS NEWS

GREAT NEW PORT PLANNED

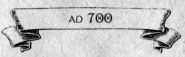
AD 700

Faster trade with Europe
Building work has begun on a new **port**. It will be called Southampton. "It's going to be the biggest trading centre in Britain," said a spokesman for King Ine of Wessex. "Bigger than York, Dublin, Ipswich – even London!"

What's so great about Southampton? For a start it is in Wessex, a powerful kingdom that covers central southern England. And the fact that Southampton is on the south coast means it is much nearer to Europe. Ships can bring goods here from the continent much more quickly.

LONDON HITS NEW HIGH

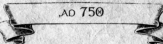
AD 750

London is not just Britain's largest city. It also has more people in it than anywhere else. The population living here is heading for an astonishing 10,000!

BUSINESS NEWS

SLAVERY IS WICKED

Bishop slams slave trade

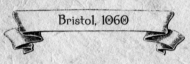

Bristol, 1060

Wulfstan, the Bishop of Worcester, has attacked the keeping of slaves. On a visit to Bristol he has argued that it is wrong to buy and sell human beings. Everyone has a right to be free, he says.

But slavery is a big business in Bristol. Irish traders come to the market here to buy shiploads of British slaves. They are taken back to Ireland and sold off to rich landowners. And there are busy slave markets in other big towns, such as London.

Will Wulfstan's words change all this? We'll have to wait and see.

Slavery facts

ᘓ One Briton in ten is a slave or **serf** – that's more than 120,000 men, women and children!

ᘓ Most slaves are British. They are criminals, prisoners captured in battle, people who can't pay their debts or who may have been born into slavery.

ᘓ Slaves may be set free when their owner dies.

ᘓ Serfs or peasants do most of the hard work on farms or in houses.

FARMING NEWS

LOTS OF CROPS

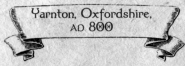

Yarnton, Oxfordshire, AD 800

by our Agricultural Editor, Don McSpreader

Some fields are green, when the grass is growing. Some are yellow, when the crops are ready to be cut down. Some are brown, when they are ploughed. But how can a field be blue?

"That's **flax**," said one of the villagers. "We grow a lot now. It's got pretty blue flowers. And you can make cloth out of the stalks."

But you can't eat them. Luckily, farmers here are also growing new kinds of food crops. There are oats and wheat, which are easier to harvest. There are yummy fruits like grapes and plums. They've also built a new shed for the geese and chickens. And plenty of pigs snuffle about in the woods.

FARMING NEWS

PLOUGH ABOUT THAT?

Ploughing in strips

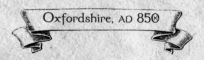

Oxfordshire, AD 850

Farmers always want more land. This lets them grow more food.

Now villagers in Oxfordshire have made a breakthrough: bigger ploughs! Their latest model is so big it needs a team of eight **oxen**.

"This plough just rips through anything,"

says local farmer Hengist Horseface. "Rocks, clay, old tree trunks. Gives me a lot more space."

But eight oxen can be hard to control and even harder to turn around. So the farmers just plough strips of land in one long straight line. The strip fields can be as long as 200 metres. That's as far as the oxen can go before they need a rest.

A Day in the Life

This week...
ROOM WITH A LOOM

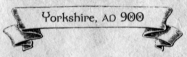
Yorkshire, AD 900

When it's sunny, Sheena Shuttle works outside. "If it's cold and wet," she says, "I can go indoors. The shed is a bit gloomy, but I'd rather be inside, safe from the wind and rain." Her husband, like most men, has to work out in the fields all year round.

Sheena is a weaver, making cloth on a big wooden frame called a **loom**. She hangs wool threads from the top of the loom. They have clay weights on the ends to keep them tight. Then she weaves more wool in and out between the hanging threads. It's slow work and the hours are long. "I start when the sun rises and stop when it's dark," she says.

LETTERS TO THE EDITOR

You tell Britain what you think

Navy? Crazy!

Why is King Alfred building lots of navy ships? It's a complete waste of money. Our brave soldiers have won all their battles on land. Anyone who thinks we'd ever have battles on the sea is just barmy.

Yours sincerely

GODRIC GRUMPY (BRIGADIER)

Hastings, 896

Why go to school?

A lot of kids these days spend their time in class being taught to read and write. What's the point? When I was a lad, I was out in the fields with my dad learning to chop wood and tend the sheep. I never went to school. It didn't do me any harm.

Yours sincerely

ETHELBALD THE HAIRY

York, 975

Pict your own

You Anglo-Saxons think you're pretty clever. You've taken over the whole of England. But remember this – you've never conquered Scotland or Ireland or even Wales. We've all got our own leaders.

Yours sincerely

FLORA McSPORRAN

Ecclefechan, 1060

CELEB NEWS

First with the latest about people who matter

COWHERD BECOMES STAR

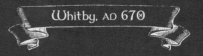

Whitby, AD 670

Caedmon was once a shy man. He hated singing. At feasts, he would run away when someone asked him to sing.

But suddenly last week something amazing happened. As usual, he had fled from a feast and gone to hide in the cow shed. Soon he fell asleep and began to dream. A man was calling him, saying "Caedmon, sing me something."

"What shall I sing?" he asked.

The man replied, "Sing about how the world was made." So in his dream, Caedmon began a beautiful song he had never heard before. When he woke up, he remembered every word. And that is how Caedmon has become a great singer and poet.

CELEB NEWS

THE KING WITH NO BONES

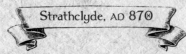

Strathclyde, AD 870

By our Viking correspondent Beorn Bonkers

King Ivar is a giant. He's terrifying. He's the strongest warrior in the land. But many people say he was born without a bone in his body.

The Viking monster has smashed his way across Britain with his great army. He has defeated the Northumbrians *and* the Scots and put to death three rival kings. How does Ivar the Boneless do it?

A Viking contact told me: "It's rubbish. Ivar has bones like anyone else. He's just amazingly supple and bendy. He can wriggle his way out of any tight spot."

QUEEN-TASTIC!

London, 1017

Fancy marrying a king? It sounds amazing. But it was not enough for Emma of Normandy. She's married TWO kings!

First, Emma wed Ethelred, England's ruler. He was a weak man. Ethelred's land was invaded by Danish prince Cnut. Then Ethelred died last year. Bad news for Emma, you might think. But no – she's gone and married Cnut. Now she's a queen twice over!

FASHION HIGHLIGHTS

BLING FOR BISHOPS

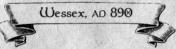
Wessex, AD 890

Beauty, by royal command. These fabulous little jewels are made of gold and crystal and shaped like a teardrop. But you can't buy one, no matter how rich you are. They are strictly for bishops. King Alfred had these jewels made and he's sending one to every church leader. They go on a long rod and become a handle for a pointer stick. You use the stick to follow words when reading a manuscript. Handy!

STUNNING SILK

London, AD 700
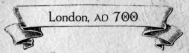

Good news! New supplies of **silk** cloth have arrived in Britain. The silk comes from Byzantium, far away in the East. The people there have learned the secret of making this wonderful material. Now here's the bad news. Silk is amazingly expensive. Hardly anyone can afford to buy it – even kings.

IF YOU WANT TO GET AHEAD, GET A SOCK

York, AD 600

Say goodbye to frozen feet. Pull on a pair of socks this winter and stay warm and clean. Socks: all the poshest people are wearing them.

HANDY HINTS

Egbert Cleverclogs answers your queries

Q: I live in Staffordshire and I've got a huge hoard of gold and silver. How can I keep it safe from these terrible Viking raiders?

A: *Dig a big hole in a field and put all your treasure in there. Cover it with earth and no one will ever find it again. Not for at least 1,300 years, anyway.*

Q: How do I make a sword? There isn't a sword shop anywhere nearby.

A: *You need big muscles and a very hot fire, for a start. And you'll need a big heavy hammer. Heat up some bars of iron then twist them together. Hammer the iron flat, then heat and hammer again. Put it in water to cool off.*

Q: I'm sick of wearing brown clothes. How can I make them in jollier colours?

A: *Cheer up! There are lots of bright coloured dyes. You can make them yourself, by finding the right plants and stewing them in a pot. **Lichen** gives reds and purples. **Woad** makes a lovely blue and **broom** makes yellow. Is that jolly enough?*

TRAVEL NEWS

SPEED BOAT

Transport writer Phil Seasick takes a ride in a Viking longship

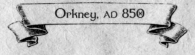
Orkney, AD 850

I'm sitting in a Viking **longship**. It's whizzing across the sea, bumping through the waves. The cloth sail bulges in the wind and the spray blows in my face.

Long and thin, the ship is built of oak planks fastened with wooden pegs. A carved dragon's head sticks up at the front.

But what if there's no wind? There are 34 burly **Norsemen** in the crew who can row with their long oars. A longship can get from Norway to Scotland in just 24 hours. No wonder we're so scared of the Vikings!

TRAVEL NEWS

WHERE'S THAT?
Place names explained

Word	Meaning	As in...
borough or burgh	town with a wall	Edinburgh
burn	stream	Blackburn
ford	shallow river crossing	Oxford
ham	village	Birmingham

KEEP OUT!

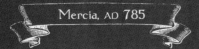
Mercia, AD 785

Want to get to Wales? It will soon be a lot harder to enter. Thousands of men are digging a huge ditch and an earth wall along the border between Mercia and Wales. The Mercian King Offa wants to keep the Welsh out. He's sick of thieves stealing his cattle.

HOMES FOR SALE

BARGAIN OF THE WEEK

Dinefwr, Carmarthen

Here's a classic wooden house in the south of Wales. Outside, it has a sturdy frame of timber and mud and stones. On top, it has a thick roof of reeds. And inside, there is one spacious room with stone fireplace. Plus: state-of-the-art hole in the roof to allow smoke to escape. How can you resist this bargain?

Price: 350 silver coins

Yeavering, Northumbria

Buy a piece of history! This field may look empty now but it was once the site of a real Great Hall. King Edwin slept and held banquets in this huge space. Then one terrible day it burned down. So here's your chance to rebuild that mighty wooden hall and live the life of a lord! There will be space for lots of people, with a giant fire in the middle for cooking and heating.

Price: 2,500 silver coins

HOMES FOR SALE

Bath, Somerset

Live like the Romans (remember them?). Buy a corner of this ancient bathhouse. OK, so it's a ruin, but you can soon make it cosy. The good news is it's built of stone so you don't have to worry about fire. And there's both hot and cold running water on site.

Price: 2 horses and 5 sheep

Mousa, Shetland Islands

Broch aye! Live the good life far from other people and next to the sea. The Mousa Broch has good thick stone walls and stands over 13 metres high. From the top you can see for many kilometres. Even the Vikings can't sneak up on you! And there's plenty of land for growing barley.

Price: 10 tonnes of herrings

FOOD AND DRINK

THE BIG FEAST:

Restaurant Review by Cnut Roast

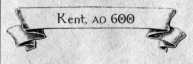

Kent, AD 600

What a noise! The long tables in the Feasting Hall at Lyminge were packed with 60 happy eaters last night – including me! All of us were busy chewing great chunks of meat and talking at the same time. There was beef, chicken, lamb, deer and rabbit, all grilled on the huge fire.

And to wash it down we had **mead** and ale. There was cabaret, too. Rapper B. Ard sang songs from his new album "Don't Go Breaking My Harp".

Rating: ✶✶✶✶✶

DRINK UP

New drinking cups are all the rage. You can't let go of them until they're empty, though. Why? Because they're made from cattle horns, which don't have a flat base. So if you put them down, they'll just fall over and spill mead everywhere.

FOOD AND DRINK

CAN DEAD PEOPLE EAT?

Can dead people really eat? Everyone is arguing about whether we should bury food next to corpses. **Pagans** say the dead get hungry just like anyone else. They need food down there in the dark. But Christians say this is wrong.

Even so, many people are still filling graves with things to eat. Here are some of the titbits being left underground:

ᵔ Duck eggs in Suffolk

ᵔ Oysters in Kent

ᵔ Chickens and geese in Yorkshire

ᵔ Lamb chops in Suffolk

ᵔ Cooked ox heads in Oxfordshire

ᵔ A whole joint of beef in Derbyshire

ᵔ Other grave grub includes hazelnuts, crab apples, wine and porridge.

ARTS AND ENTERTAINMENT

....Book news...........Book news...........Book news...........Boo

HEROES AND MONSTERS

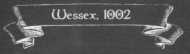
Wessex, 1002

Beowulf is a blockbuster. This thrilling and bloodthirsty tale of a great warrior and his battles will keep you on the edge of your seat.

The story begins when Beowulf is told about a savage monster called Grendel. This monster comes out of the marshes every night. He goes to the Great Hall to kill and eat a soldier. One night, Beowulf lies in wait and grabs Grendel. There is an epic fight, and Grendel crawls away to die. But this is just the beginning. For Grendel has a mother, who is even more terrifying…

Beowulf is available now. You can get it as a book printed on animal skin (Bogeyman Press, 12 silver pennies). Or, if you like live readings, you can hear it read at a **mead hall** near you.

ARTS AND ENTERTAINMENT

s............Book news............Book news.......Book news.........

IRISH BEAUTY

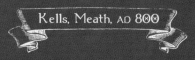

Kells, Meath, AD 800

Is it a book – or is it a work of art? The *Book of Kells* is both. It is also one of the most beautiful things in Britain today. It was created by monks in Scotland and Ireland. Inside are the four Gospels from the Bible, which tell the story of Jesus's life.

So what's so amazing about it? Well, the hand-written words are lit up by wonderful paintings. There are pictures of Jesus and Mary and saints and angels. Dozens of animals appear. Cats chase mice among the words and an otter eats a fish. Moths fly and plants wind round the words. Best of all are the bright colours of the clever designs and patterns.

Just as amazing is the story of the book itself. It was begun on the island of Iona. But when the Vikings attacked the island the monks had to flee. They sailed to Ireland, taking the *Book of Kells* with them.

FOR SALE

HOUSEHOLD

Comb
Say goodbye to tangled hair. Made from genuine bone.

Genuine Viking sword
Double-edged and very sharp! The best you can get. (Note from seller: Beware! Dangerous object!)

Pair of trousers
Made in Scotland, as worn by the Picts. One careful owner. In good condition, except for small arrow hole.

Walrus tusk
Brought back by an explorer in the far North. Beautifully carved.

How to Bake Cakes by Alfred the Great
Rare copy of this ground-breaking cookbook by King Alfred himself.

FARM AND GARDEN

20 sheep fleeces
Fresh off the sheep's backs. Can be used to make strong

wool thread.

1 sack of acorns
Your pigs will love them. And they

make the meat taste even yummier.

Wooden rake
Second-hand, but with all its own teeth. Perfect for collecting the hay.

SERVICES

Find that gold!
Buried your treasure and can't remember where? Call in Hoard Busters! We're the experts in riches recovery.

Cuthbert the Carver
Perfect for all your stone carving needs. Dragons are a speciality.

Basket weaving course
Learn to make your own baskets on this two-day course run by Jekka McWicker.

Rune service
Are you puzzled by mysterious marks on rocks? Our **Norse** workers will examine the runes and tell you what they mean.

Jobs

Make money!
Workers wanted for new Dublin **mint**. Must have experience in producing silver pennies.

Ploughboy needed
Hitch up your ox team and plough the fields. Hours: dawn till dusk, six days a week. Very low pay.

Get in the habit
Train to be a monk and go to church seven times a day. Long hours, no pay, but spiritual rewards and lots of good food.

Anglian Ales
We're looking for a new head brewer to make our beer. Only women need apply.

TIMELINE

AD 400

AD 410
Roman army leaves Britain

AD 450
Angles, Saxons and Jutes begin to settle in Britain

AD 500
Scots and Irish found kingdom of Dalriada

AD 680
Most of North Scotland now ruled by the Picts

AD 630
Gold and silver "hoard" buried in Staffordshire

AD 620
Ship burial of Raedwald at Sutton Hoo, Suffolk

AD 597
The Pope sends priests to convert the Anglo-Saxons to Christianity

AD 700
Building work in Southampton establishes the town as a major Wessex **port**

AD 785
King Offa of Mercia builds a ditch along his border with Wales

AD 793
Vikings raid the holy island of Lindisfarne

AD 800
The *Book of Kells* is created

AD 850
Bigger ploughs allow farmers to use rough land for crops

AD 896
King Alfred is thought by many to have founded Britain's first navy

AD 878
Alfred defeats the **Danes** at the Battle of Edington and drives them out of Wessex

AD 945
Most of Wales unites for the first time under King Hywel Dda

AD 970
Slave markets flourish in London, Bristol and Ireland

AD 1000

c.1002
The epic poem *Beowulf* is written down for the first time

1006
Norse invaders settle in most parts of Britain and Ireland

1066
William of Normandy becomes King of England

GLOSSARY

ancestor person we are descended from (such as a mother or a great-great-grandfather)

broch round stone tower found in Scotland

bronze metal made by mixing copper and tin

broom plant with yellow flowers, from which we make yellow dye

Dane person from Denmark

flax plant whose stems can be used to make linen cloth

Gaelic language of the Gaels, who lived in Ireland and Scotland

Gaul ancient region of Europe. The area covers modern-day France, Belgium, south-west Germany, the southern Netherlands and north Italy.

lichen small plant that grows on rocks and trees; it is used to make red dyes for cloth

longship narrow and fast-moving vessel used by the Vikings

loom wooden frame used for weaving cloth

mead alcoholic drink made from honey

mead hall place for feasting and drinking, like a modern-day pub

mint place where coins are made

monastery religious centre where monks live and work

Norse Norwegians from Norway or Scandinavians from Iceland and Sweden during ancient times

oxen male cattle, used to pull ploughs

pagan person holding religious beliefs other than those of the main world religions. In Anglo-Saxon Britain, a Christian would call a non-Christian a pagan.

port seaside town with a harbour for loading and unloading cargo (goods)

serf worker, or labourer, who worked on a landowner's lands. The serf was tied to the land there in exchange for freedom but had the right to grow his or her own food.

silk smooth, shiny fabric made from fibres produced by silkworms

woad plant whose leaves are used to make blue dye

FIND OUT MORE

There's a lot more to find out about the Anglo-Saxons, the Picts and all the other people mentioned in this book. And new discoveries are being made all the time. Read about them in books or online, or visit some of the hundreds of great buildings and other sites from the period. Here's just a tiny selection to get you started.

BOOKS

Anglo-Saxons, Jane Bingham (Wayland, 2015)

Anglo-Saxon and Viking Britain, Alex Woolf (Franklin Watts, 2012)

Beowulf, Michael Morpurgo (Walker Books, 2013)

Britain's Settlement by the Anglo-Saxons and Scots (Early British History), Claire Throp (Raintree, 2016)

Life in Anglo-Saxon Britain (A Child's History of Britain), Anita Ganeri (Raintree, 2015)

WEBSITES

www.bbc.co.uk/education/topics/zxsbcdm
This BBC website gives lots of information through videos, animations and lots more.

www.ngkids.co.uk/history/anglo-saxons
This National Geographic website has lots of fascinating information about the Anglo-Saxons.

www.primaryhomeworkhelp.co.uk/saxons.htm
This website gives the answers to the big questions about the Saxons.

PLACES TO VISIT IN GREAT BRITAIN AND IRELAND

All these places or artefacts are mentioned in this book. Is there one near you?

Alfred Jewel
Ashmolean Museum, Oxford, Oxfordshire OX1 2PH
See the most famous of all Anglo-Saxon discoveries.

The Book of Kells
Trinity College, Dublin 2, Ireland
The book is on display in Trinity College Library.

Holy Island, Lindisfarne
Berwick-upon-Tweed, Northumberland TD15 2RX
You can cross to the island when the tide is out!

Mousa Broch
Mousa, Shetland ZE2 9HP
Look inside the ancient round tower.

Offa's Dyke
Offa's Dyke Centre, Knighton, Powys LD7 1EN
Offa's Dyke is around 285 kilometres long!

Sutton Hoo
Woodbridge, Suffolk IP12 3DJ
You can see the burial mounds and reproductions of the Sutton Hoo finds.

INDEX